MAGGIE ADERIN-POCOCK:

SPACE SCIENTIST

Jo Nelson

Illustrated by **Charley Fears**

CONTENTS

WHO AM I?

My name is Maggie Aderin-Pocock and I am a space scientist who loves to share my passion for science with everyone.

I also build complex machinery to send into space. This helps us to understand our planet and the universe around us.

This means that I get to travel across the country and around the world, giving lectures and making television programmes that explain my ideas about science.

Being black and female means people are sometimes surprised that I am a scientist, but it is the job I dreamed of as a child. Since I was young I have always wanted to travel into space. It was a mad idea for a **dyslexic** kid sitting at the back of the class at school! It was inspired by a children's programme that I used to watch and it's an idea that has made a real difference to my life.

I might not have reached my goal of getting to space yet but I am still hopeful. I have found that by having such a far out, crazy dream I have been driven to achieve much more than I would have thought possible as a child!

In my life so far I have met Queen Elizabeth II and travelled many times around the world with my daughter. I have worked on systems that **detect** landmines (bombs that can hurt children and adults), and I have built machines that look into the hearts of distant stars.

I would love to share my story so that it might inspire you to not give up on your own dream, no matter what it is. I hope that you have as much fun trying to achieve your dream as I have. Happy adventures!

Maggie

A MOON BABY

At the age of three, Maggie sat watching a children's animated television show called *Clangers*, and fell in love with space. She was fascinated by the idea of other worlds and desperately wanted to explore them for herself.

The Clangers are a fictional family of mouse-like creatures who live on a peaceful, distant planet. Each episode of *Clangers* invites the viewers to travel across the endless stretches of outer space using their imaginations.

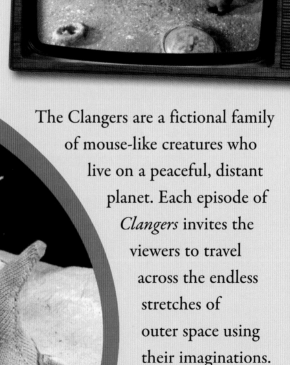

Maggie was born in north London in 1968. Her parents were Nigerian and Maggie was the third of their four daughters. When Maggie was four years old, her parents divorced. The break-up was difficult for everyone, but Maggie found her own way of coping. She would use her imagination and escape into space.

The Clangers weren't Maggie's only source of inspiration. Around the time Maggie was born, the first mission to send people to the Moon was being planned. In 1969, as Maggie was taking her first wobbly steps, Neil Armstrong and Buzz Aldrin were taking a massive leap for mankind. As Maggie toddled about, the images and excitement of the Moon landings were all around her.

As Maggie grew older, there was another television programme that she loved to watch: *Star Trek*. She eagerly followed the adventures of the starship *Enterprise*. The crew's mission was to boldly go where no man had gone before. Maggie decided that was where she was going too.

> 66 *I find the Moon* **mesmerizing**. *It's probably a nasty place to live – there's no* **atmosphere** *and you'd have to walk around in space suits all the time – but at the same time it's so beautiful!* 99

AIMING HIGH

Throughout her childhood, the mysteries of the night sky were a welcome distraction for Maggie. When her parents split up, they couldn't agree on where their daughters should live. Maggie found herself moving around London from one house to another. She ended up going to 13 different schools in 14 years.

On top of that, Maggie was finding it hard to read and write, and at the age of eight she was diagnosed with dyslexia.

> **"** *I found school very frustrating. At home I felt quite bright but with the reading and writing I felt very dumb in the classroom. Things that the kids around me did with ease, I found very difficult.* **"**

Maggie would sit at the back of the class, not enjoying lessons at all. The one thing that got her excited was the idea of space travel. When a teacher asked Maggie what she wanted to be when she grew up, she instantly replied, "An astronaut!"

At that time, in the 1970s, only one woman had ever been in space. It seemed very unlikely that little Maggie would ever become an astronaut. "Why don't you be a nurse instead?" the teacher suggested.

Maggie's mother had other ideas. She thought that Maggie should be an actress!

> 66 *Space appealed to me because life seemed very challenging on Earth at times.* 99

WOMEN IN SPACE

1963 ──● Valentina Tereshkova is the first woman in space.

1982 ──● Nearly 20 years go by before another woman, Svetlana Savitskaya, goes into space.

On her second space ──● **1984** mission, Savitskaya is the first woman to walk in space.

1991 ●── The first British person in space is a woman, Helen Sharman.

Mae Jemison is the first black woman to ──● **1992** go into space.

Reading and writing might have been hard for Maggie, but that didn't stop her from asking questions.

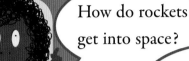

How do rockets get into space?

How does the Earth move?

How many other planets are there?

Maggie would pester her father with questions, but he didn't always have an answer. Instead, he would take her to the library to find out more.

In the 1970s, when Maggie was a child, you couldn't just go online to answer a question. Most families didn't own a computer, and the Internet wasn't available for everyday use until the 1990s. So Maggie would come home armed with a pile of books and leaf through them.

Education was very important to Maggie's father. He had moved from Nigeria to England with the dream of becoming a doctor, but it hadn't worked out. That was one of his biggest disappointments in life. His other big disappointment was not having a son. Maggie decided she could fill that gap. "I'll be a boy like no other boy," she told him.

Maggie's father hoped that his daughter might study medicine, but Maggie had no intention of being a doctor. She was, however, beginning to discover a talent for science.

The turning point for Maggie came one day at school when she was about 10. Maggie was in her usual place at the back of the class and her teacher was asking a question.

If 1 litre of water weighs 1 kilogram, how much will 1 cubic centimetre weigh?

$\square = 1KG$

$1 cm^3 = ?$

The answer seemed obvious to Maggie. Her hand shot up, but no one else's did. Maggie almost put her hand down again, but decided to give it a go.

1 gram?

Yes!

> *That was a real turning point for me. I couldn't believe that dumb Maggie sitting at the back could get the question right.*

SEEING THE STARS

Maggie became more and more interested in science. She would read about it at school and continue reading about it at home. Her enthusiasm spread to other subjects too and her work began to improve. When Maggie next moved schools, she was asked which class she should be in. "The top one," she replied. No one questioned her and she got on fine.

Through studying science, Maggie was finding out how the world works and how people make new discoveries. She decided to become a scientist herself, and the first thing she wanted to study was ... the stars!

Stargazing in a city isn't easy. Even on a clear night, the **light pollution** from street lamps, buildings and traffic could stop her from seeing the stars above. So Maggie would seek out big, open spaces, away from **artificial** light. As a teenager, Maggie's favourite walk home was through Hampstead Heath, one of London's biggest parks. Here, the city lights faded and the stars shone bright.

At the age of 15, Maggie saved up her pocket money and bought her first telescope. She aimed it at the night sky, but the image was all blurry. To Maggie's dismay, she discovered that the telescope didn't work properly. Then she spotted an advert in a magazine ...

I'll make a better telescope!

MAKE YOUR OWN
TELESCOPE
ADULT EVENING CLASSES
SIGN UP NOW!

Over the following months, Maggie learned how to carefully grind her own mirror and construct her very own telescope.

" To create it myself and make the craters on the Moon jump out was magical. "

MAGGIE'S TELESCOPE

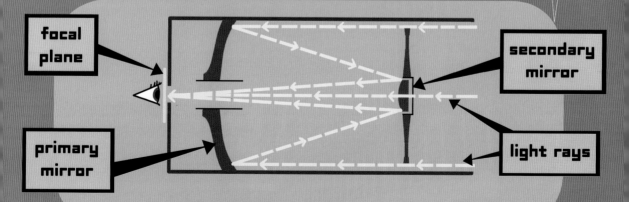

focal plane

secondary mirror

primary mirror

light rays

MAKING THE GRADE

By the age of 16, Maggie knew she definitely wanted to go to university after she'd finished school. There was so much more to learn! She studied physics, chemistry, biology and maths in her final two years at school, then got a university place at Imperial College London to study physics.

As a child, Maggie had walked past the university buildings many times, on the way to visit the Science Museum with her father. Now, aged 18, she was walking through the door as a student.

> " To me, physics is the study of everything, from the smallest **particles** known to man to the edge of the universe. And I'm really inquisitive, so it was just the subject for me. "

Maggie briefly imagined herself using mathematics to come up with amazing new **theories** about the universe. In reality, she was much more suited to practical experiments. She preferred working with her hands and seeing things with her own eyes.

Maggie specialized in optics – the study of light and instruments that use light, such as telescopes. She decided to study for a further qualification, called a PhD, in **mechanical engineering**, so she could find other uses for optics. In Maggie's PhD studies she used light to measure very thin layers of engine oil. She used her measurements to decide which oils would work best in which engines.

The light we can see all around us is known as visible light. It can be separated out into the colours of the rainbow. Then there's light that we can't see, such as infrared and ultraviolet. The different kinds of light form part of the **electromagnetic spectrum**.

By studying the way light travels, we can find out more about how things work, both on Earth and in space.

BEING JAMES BOND

It was a proud day for Maggie's whole family when she finished her PhD and became Dr Maggie Aderin. Now she needed to find a job where she could put her seven years of university study to good use.

Maggie was invited for an interview with the Ministry of Defence (MoD). The MoD is the part of the British government that is responsible for the country's army, navy and air force. Maggie impressed her interviewers and was offered a job ... only they wouldn't tell her what the job involved until she accepted it. She even had to sign the Official Secrets Act, which meant promising not to give away any government secrets.

Maggie decided to risk it. She began work at the MoD and discovered that her job was to invent a **missile** warning system for pilots. Before long, Maggie found herself hanging out of the door of a plane, high in the sky, taking photos of missiles. She needed to know what approaching missiles looked like, so she could find a way for her missile warning system to detect them.

FACT FILE

A missile warning system is fixed to the outside of a plane. When it detects a missile it lets off a big, hot flare. Because missiles use heat to track down planes, the missile follows the flare instead of the plane. Meanwhile, the pilot can fly to safety.

Maggie found the job rewarding. She was glad to get the chance to save lives with her warning system, but she felt uncomfortable that other people were using science to make weapons. Working for the MoD wasn't what she'd imagined herself doing after university, but it was a good first job and there were more exciting experiences to come.

> "As a scientist I expected I'd be in a lab somewhere, playing around with test tubes, but this was more like being James Bond!"

FINDING HER VOICE

In 1997, Maggie was promoted within the MoD to lead a team working on landmine detection. Maggie's team was tasked with designing a handheld device that would detect landmines so they could be removed before they injured anyone.

FACT FILE

Landmines are bombs hidden in the ground which explode when somebody steps on them.

Maggie's brief:

Design a landmine detection device.

It needs to be:
— light enough to carry
— cheap to make
— able to run on very little power
— able to tell the difference between old drinks cans and landmines.

It must include:
— a metal detector
— a **radar** that looks into the ground
— an explosives detector.

The project was a huge challenge, but one that Maggie rose to with enthusiasm. Once again, she was using science to save lives.

> 66 *Science affects our society in so many different ways. It's important that we understand the power of science so we can make decisions on how we want to use it.* 99

There was a lot of public interest in landmines at the time and Maggie was asked to talk about her work with politicians and journalists. Maggie discovered she had a gift for describing complicated scientific ideas in a clear and simple way. This was a skill that she would put to good use later on in life.

THE RAINBOWS OF STARS

Maggie hadn't lost sight of her dream to work in space one day. In 1999, she was asked to work on an instrument for the Gemini South telescope in Chile. Maggie jumped at the chance. She wouldn't be working *in* space, but at least she'd be collecting information *from* space.

The Gemini Observatory has two telescopes: the Gemini North in Hawaii and the Gemini South in Chile. Together they can study the whole sky.

The mirrors for each telescope are an impressive 8 metres across. That's over 50 times bigger than the one I made as a teenager.

USA

Gemini North – Hawaii

South America

Gemini South – Chile

The Gemini telescopes collect a huge amount of light. It would be too dangerous to look directly at the light through an eyepiece. Instead, the light is gathered and sent through different instruments for closer study. One instrument, called a spectrograph, separates the light into the different parts of the electromagnetic spectrum.

Effectively, the spectrograph makes rainbows. It takes the starlight from billions of miles away, puts it through various optics, then stretches the light out into its rainbow colours. From that, scientists can work out what's happening in the heart of a star.

Think of a telescope as a light-gathering bucket. The bigger the bucket, the more light you can gather, so you can see further out and detect fainter objects.

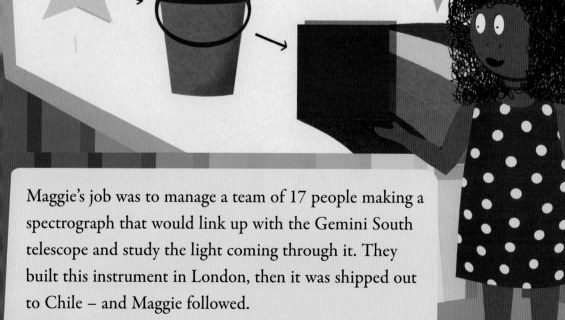

Maggie's job was to manage a team of 17 people making a spectrograph that would link up with the Gemini South telescope and study the light coming through it. They built this instrument in London, then it was shipped out to Chile – and Maggie followed.

A CATHEDRAL TO SCIENCE

The Gemini South telescope is up in the Andes Mountains, in Chile. It's an isolated place, miles from any towns, where it can get a clear view of the night sky. There are very few clouds and it's high above sea level. This means there is less interference from the Earth's atmosphere when looking out to space.

Maggie spent six months working with the telescope. She lived on her own in a little bungalow on the mountain. Although she missed her family, she didn't feel lonely. Maggie had the stars for company and she sat down every evening for dinner with the Moon.

> " As the sun set you could see amazing stars appear and it just made my heart sing. "

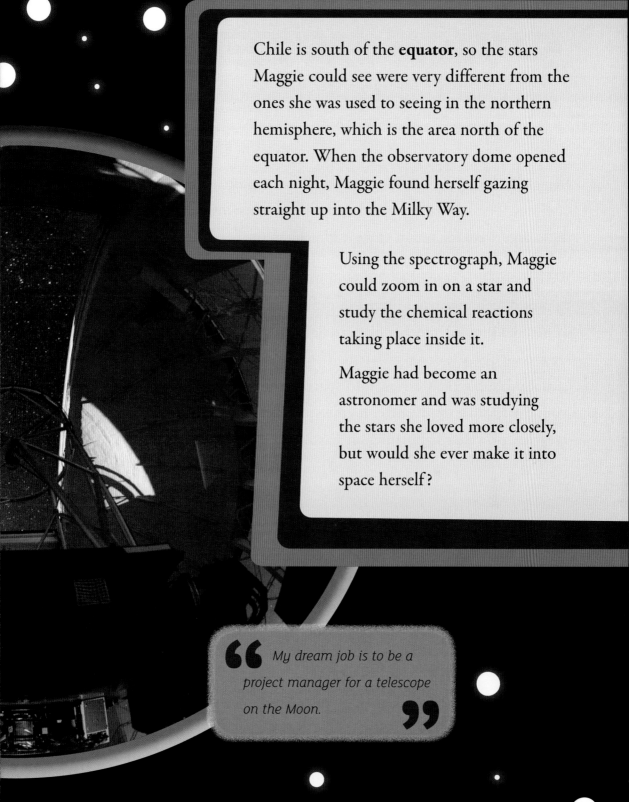

Chile is south of the **equator**, so the stars Maggie could see were very different from the ones she was used to seeing in the northern hemisphere, which is the area north of the equator. When the observatory dome opened each night, Maggie found herself gazing straight up into the Milky Way.

Using the spectrograph, Maggie could zoom in on a star and study the chemical reactions taking place inside it.

Maggie had become an astronomer and was studying the stars she loved more closely, but would she ever make it into space herself?

My dream job is to be a project manager for a telescope on the Moon.

SPACE SATELLITES

Maggie's next career move was to work for a company that made satellites. The job still involved designing science instruments, but these ones were for use in space, rather than on Earth.

We use satellites to gather and send information. They are launched into space and placed in orbit around the Earth (or sometimes around another planet). Satellites can either look out into space or back down at Earth. The advantage of being in orbit is that there is a clearer view into space without any interference from the Earth's atmosphere. It's also possible to have a better overview of what's happening on Earth.

Weather satellites look back at our planet and monitor the Earth's weather and climate.

Space telescopes are satellites that look deep into space and collect information about the universe.

The Hubble Space Telescope has been taking amazing images of space since its launch in 1990.

The Spitzer Space Telescope, launched in 2003, detects infrared light.

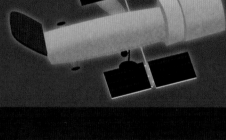

Navigation satellites are used to track planes, ships and sometimes submarines.

Communication satellites are used to beam information to phones, radios and televisions.

LOOKING DEEPER INTO SPACE

One of Maggie's satellite projects was designing part of the James Webb Space Telescope. This should eventually replace both the Hubble and the Spitzer telescopes which are currently out in space. The instrument Maggie worked on was called the Mid-Infrared Instrument, for measuring infrared light.

Infrared light is not a light that we can see, but it can travel very long distances through space. By finding and measuring infrared light, we can peer even further into outer space and learn more about what's out there.

Here are some aims for the Mid-Infrared Instrument:
- **to find out how distant galaxies are moving**
- **to discover newly forming stars**
- **to identify distant objects and what they're made of.**

For Maggie, designing new technology that can reach further into space and make new discoveries is extremely exciting. Recent results from other telescopes have included finding new planets in our galaxy. According to Maggie, these planets may well have alien life on them.

Maggie reckons aliens could be as big as a football pitch and have an orange underbelly for **camouflage**. They might also have gas-filled bags that dangle underneath them to help them float along.

Her vision is a far cry from the friendly pink Clangers, but it is based firmly on science. Unfortunately the vast distances between Earth and the planets outside our solar system mean we are unlikely to ever meet Maggie's aliens. It would take thousands of years to reach them. That's why searching for signs of life with powerful telescopes is the closest that Maggie can get.

LOOKING BACK AT EARTH

Another of Maggie's satellite projects is a weather satellite called Aeolus (*say* ee-oh-lus). It's part of the European Space Agency's Living Planet Programme, which makes detailed observations of Earth from space.

The Aeolus Satellite will measure the wind around the world for three years. The information it collects will help to make our weather forecasts more accurate. Scientists will then be able to give people more warning about extreme weather events such as hurricanes and typhoons.

Scientists believe that the greenhouse gases we are releasing into the atmosphere, through burning fossil fuels such as coal and gas, are adding to the problem of global warming. The Aeolus Satellite should tell us more about how pollution is affecting our weather and how the Earth's climate is changing.

Weather is all interconnected. Lightning storms in Ethiopia can be linked with hurricanes in the Americas. So if you understand the wind, you can actually see how it affects the bigger picture.

SPREADING THE WORD

In 2006, Maggie was asked by a British science organization to spend two days a week telling people about her work. They would pay her to share her enthusiasm for science and space by giving talks and interviews.

Maggie happily agreed. Everywhere she went, she impressed people with her energy and the vivid descriptions of her work. Soon newspaper editors, television reporters and radio presenters were asking Maggie to share her expert space knowledge with them.

Before this, Maggie had discovered a talent for explaining her work to politicians. Now she was enjoying talking to all kinds of people, particularly children. She remembered the difficulties she had faced at school. Now she could give hope and encouragement to children who had struggled like her.

Maggie set up her own company, Science Innovation Ltd, and began offering 'Tours of the Universe' to schools around the country. She would visit each school and, using computer images, take the pupils on a journey through space.

By talking about her exciting work, Maggie hoped that she could inspire children to want to become scientists themselves.

> 66 *I try to answer three questions: why I became a scientist, how I became a scientist and, most importantly, what I do as a scientist. One of the problems is that physics careers are not very visible. If you do medicine or accountancy you know what people do. I try to show them what you can do with a degree in physics.* 99

In 2009, Maggie was awarded an MBE (Member of the Order of the British Empire) by Queen Elizabeth II for her work in science and education.

A TV STAR!

In 2010, Maggie was invited by the BBC to present a television **documentary** called *Do We Really Need the Moon?* Maggie was delighted. There was only one problem. She had just had a baby! For the filming, Maggie would need to travel to different places around the world, but there was no way she would leave her daughter, Lauren, behind.

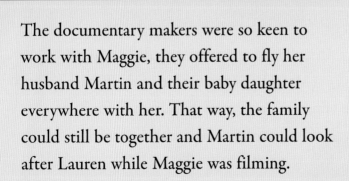

The documentary makers were so keen to work with Maggie, they offered to fly her husband Martin and their baby daughter everywhere with her. That way, the family could still be together and Martin could look after Lauren while Maggie was filming.

When asked to do talks at universities or science events, Maggie would now appear with little Lauren on her hip. Sometimes Lauren would chew on the microphone or dribble on Maggie's shirt! Maggie would just laugh and include Lauren in her explanations. She hadn't let being black or dyslexic or a woman hold her back, and now she wasn't going to let being a mum hold her back either.

Maggie's lively presenting and clear explanations about space and science made her popular with the people watching her on TV too. In 2011 she won the New Talent award from the organization Women in Film and Television. She was asked to present another documentary called *How Satellites Rule Our World*, which was first broadcast in 2012. Two years later, she became a presenter for the BBC television series, *The Sky at Night*.

Maggie may not be how most people envisage a space scientist – even the Queen was surprised when Maggie told her what she actually did – but by being herself and following her dream, she's inspiring others to do the same.

REACH FOR THE STARS

Have you ever had a crazy dream about something you'd love to do, but it seemed impossible to achieve? Hold on to that dream! Let it grow inside you and help it to develop – you never know where it might lead you.

Here's Maggie's lists of Dos and Don'ts for following your dreams:

DON'T ...

* ever think you're not good enough
* worry what other people think and say
* panic if your life takes an unexpected turn
* forget to enjoy the journey, even if you never quite reach your dream
* give up.

DO ...

- ✳ **have crazy dreams**
- ✳ **ask lots of questions**
- ✳ **find inspiration in the people and things around you, such as television programmes, websites, fictional characters and real people**
- ✳ **find out more about your passions by reading and learning and asking MORE questions**
- ✳ **make the most of opportunities that come your way**
- ✳ **believe in yourself.**

I haven't given up on my dream. I want to retire to Mars. Some people choose gardening, I choose Mars. What's your dream? And what other exciting things might happen to you while you follow your dream?

GLOSSARY

artificial: not natural; man-made

atmosphere: gases that surround Earth

camouflage: using similar colours to blend into the background

detect: find or pick out

documentary: a fact-based television programme

dyslexic: having dyslexia, which is a difficulty with reading

electromagnetic spectrum: the range of different waves of energy, including visible light, radio waves, gamma rays and X-rays

equator: the imaginary circle around the middle of the Earth, halfway between the North Pole and the South Pole

light pollution: a lightening of the night sky that makes viewing stars and planets harder – usually happens in cities with lots of bright lights

mechanical engineering: the area of science and technology that deals with the design, construction and use of machines

mesmerizing: fascinating

missile: a weapon that is launched into the sky

particles: very small specks of stuff, invisible to the human eye

radar: a device that locates something using radio waves

theories: suggested explanations of how things work

INDEX

About the Author

I'm a children's author with a passion for space – that's why this book was perfect for me. Researching Maggie's story has been really inspiring. I've now bought my daughter her first telescope so that we can study the Moon and stars together.

As well as writing books, I run creative writing workshops in primary schools. I love the way that children are so naturally imaginative and inquisitive. I certainly hope that I never stop asking questions and daring to dream.

When I'm not writing, I like drinking coffee in quirky cafes, riding my bike, and camping in the countryside where the night sky sparkles with unexplored stars.

Greg Foot, Series Editor

I've loved science ever since the day I took my papier mâché volcano into school. I filled it with far too much baking powder, vinegar and red food colouring, and WHOOSH! I covered the classroom ceiling in red goo. Now I've got the best job in the world: I present TV shows for the BBC, answer kids' science questions on YouTube, and make huge explosions on stage at festivals!

Working on TreeTops inFact has been great fun. There are so many brilliant books, and guess what ... they're all packed full of awesome facts! What's your favourite?